Fenced In:
Fighting for Freedom

Written by:
April Barber

Cadmus Publishing
www.cadmuspublishing.com

Copyright © 2021 April Barber

Published by Cadmus Publishing
www.cadmuspublishing.com
Port Angeles, WA

ISBN: 978-1-63751-154-1

All rights reserved. Copyright under Berne Copyright Convention, Universal Copyright Convention, and Pan-American Copyright Convention. No part of this book may be reproduced, stored in a retrieval system, or transmitted in any form, or by any means, electronic, mechanical, photocopying, recording or otherwise, without prior permission of the author.

"Don't talk about what you're gonna do…
Talk about what you did."

Contents

1	1
2	3
3	5
4	6
5	8
6	10
7	12
8	14
9	16
10	18
11	20
12	22
13	24
14	26
15	27
16	29
17	31
18	33
19	36
20	38
21	41
22	43
23	45
24	47
25	49
26	50
27	52
28	54
29	56
30	58
31	60
32	62
33	64
34	65
35	67
36	69

37	70
38	71
39	72
40	74
41	76
42	78
43	80
44	82
45	84
46	86
47	88
48	89
49	91
50	92
51	93
52	95
53	97
54	99
55	100
56	102
57	103
58	105
59	106
60	108
61	110
62	112
63	114
64	116
66	118
67	120
68	122
69	123
70	125
71	126
72	127
73	128
74	129
75	130

1

Sometimes the only place to start is at the bottom. I've been at the bottom for so long that I may not recognize it when I rise above the ashes.

I was born in 1975 to a teenage mother named Sheila who was still a child herself. Sheila was adopted by Aaron and Lillie, who could not have children of their own. Aaron and Lillie gave Sheila a chance to get her life together and hopefully gravitate towards motherhood—that never happened. In 1978 my grandparents officially became my parents. I remember seeing a picture of me in a bassinette and in black and white. Damn, I'm getting old.

My earliest memories begin at age three. I remember watching Aaron doodle chickens and color their eyes red. Who knows why he did that because we didn't have a farm. Perhaps he grew up on one. I also remember reading the newspaper and watching "60 Minutes." Aaron would randomly call out a word to challenge my cognition. Not to brag, but I always got them right. Knowledge made me feel empowered. I emulated what I saw my grandparents do. Lillie was a phenomenal cook, especially with desserts. Meals never came out of a box. We gardened and canned everything. Life seemed so simple when I was little.

My birthday is in November, so I started school late. School wasn't the problem. I didn't think that I had to go without my grandparents. My bookbag was ready and filled with a bunch of shit that was totally irrelevant to kindergarten. I was excited for my first day until I realized that Lillie was about to leave me. I don't know if you've ever heard the expression "cut the fool" but that's exactly what I did. I grabbed Lillie's leg, whom I affectionately called Ma, and pleaded for dear life to not be left alone. "Ma, don't leave me! Ma, I'm sick!" I cried so badly that I literally made myself sick. I never made it a full day on the first week. I eventually calmed down and truly began to love school.

Lillie worked for a prominent doctor and his family. She was a housekeeper. The Bundy's seemed nice and thought that I was as cute as a button. Well duh, I still am.

2

Although Sheila was their daughter, she wasn't around until she had no place to be. Sheila married at 19 to a man who was 42. Lillie said that she married to get out of the house. Sheila said that she married for love. Buddy had a small daughter. Who in the world thought that it was a good idea for Sheila to be a stepmother when she detested the idea of being a mother? Sheila had absolutely no maternal instincts.

I read a lot and I suppose was somewhat introverted. There were few children in the neighborhood. and I never felt like I clicked with people my age. Aaron was my playmate and best friend. He nicknamed me "Boy" and taught me how to tie my shoes, bat, bike, etc. I was rough around the edges. Some things never change. I developed a love for art probably from Aaron's chickens. There was an art gallery at the bottom of the hill where Lillie worked. I took art classes three days a week studying Picasso, Rembrandt, and Van Gogh.

Once when Sheila and Buddy visited, I was playing in the glove compartment to their car before Buddy set it on fire to get the insurance. I came across a hypodermic needle. Buddy's sister Peggy was diabetic, so it was easily dismissed as being odd. This began one of many of Sheila's secrets and lies. The needle was Sheila's, and she was on drugs, heroin to be exact. I was eight years old. First I'm adopted. Now my mother's a drug addict. Gee, thanks, universe.

I excelled scholastically. I loved school and I was good at it. I only participated in sports when it was mandatory. I still don't play well with others.

Sheila was overweight and so was my teenage dad, Sandy. Harvey is his name, but his hair is sandy-colored. Henceforth the sobriquet. I've never gone hungry and had no rules as for what I could or couldn't eat. Along with my terrible "fat genes" I became an obese child. I suffered in silence for many years about my body. Honestly, I still and will always want to lose that magic 10 pounds.

3

Sheila's drug issues began to surface in the form of her stealing to maintain her high. Sheila was a college study CNA and was brilliant. She chose to use her hands and not her head to get what she wanted in life. Sheila boosted, forged signatures, and slept around to get money. She had such a good upbringing. I still wonder what went wrong. I was forgotten at times due to Sheila's wild life. I lacked emotionally because my grandparents were tending to Sheila's issues and secretly wondering where they went wrong as parents. It wasn't them. This was Sheila's mess. I wish that they were around so I could tell them that.

I was not a sickly child, but I do recall having strep throat and walking pneumonia. I had a fever of 104 degrees. It broke and I didn't have to be admitted into the hospital. I also remember the dentist. I like the dentist, but I do not know why I'm not terrified of him. I had a baby tooth pulled and that S.O.B. put his knee in my chest to pull it out. Really. That was necessary?

4

Boredom is a terrible thing for a child. I would often finish my work and soon became the class clown. Ms. Crowe was the sweetest kindergarten teacher in the world even when she made me stay after school writing, "I will not..." on the blackboard.

First grade was pretty much like kindergarten except for my midget teacher Ms. Hill. For real. I shit you not. She was a midget. She had rickets as a child and was as evil as she was tall. We had corporal punishment back then. Ms. Hill bent my hand back and hit it with this thick-ass paddle and broke a blood vessel. When I got home, I showed Ma, who in turn showed Dr. Bundy. Ma went to school, cussed Ms. Hill out (not literally), and needless to say, that was the last of my school punishments. Lillie did not play that shit. Middle finger to you, Ms. Hill.

School was the escape and distraction that I needed from home. I learned a lot about having good work ethics, paying bills, and taking care of your house inside and out. I was lonely, though. I wanted a friend. I wanted my mother. Sheila promised to come to church. Sheila promised to visit. Sheila promised... The promises began to go in one ear and out the other like the hopes I had of ever having a relationship with her.

    I attended the same school from kindergarten to the eighth grade. That's a long time to be around the same people. My second-grade teacher was a cousin of Aaron's. She was strict but you knew what Ms. Butler expected of you and didn't deviate. I won a lot of spelling bees and recited "The Night Before Christmas" in church for the first time. It became a tradition for many years. I was made to go to church. It wasn't a terrible thing and I'm not opposed to it when children are small until they can figure out who they are, their beliefs, etc. I was steadily going to church, yet God never showed up.

5

Sandy was a bit of a wild child. He actually still is. He lies about his age and chases women. At some point he married, but that doesn't slow him down. Sandy is a hazel/green-eyed Indian with a temper. He and my uncle Bobby got into a bit of trouble around my third-grade year. That bit of trouble consisted of second-degree murder.

Even though I'm adopted, the rural community knows everyone and everyone's business. Their crime was plastered over the news and the stares and whispers began. I became even more withdrawn for fear of being shunned. I avoided people because I felt as though they avoided me. Unless I am the leader I still dodge as many people as possible. I'm definitely not afraid of being alone.

The "Encyclopedia Britannica" was one of my favorite things to read. The clear sections of the body mesmerized me. I developed a love for the human body—well, everyone's except my own.

My fourth-grade teacher was a robust woman named Ms. Bumgarner. She left the room to make copies and forbade us to move. Among other classroom antics, my fat ass got stuck in one of those wooden desks with the hole on the bottom for books. I was spinning around on my side trying to get up. I finally got up. Everyone was laughing. It was awful and humiliating. I did what every fat kid would've done—I screamed, "All of y'all go straight to hell!" and ran to the bathroom in tears. I wore an 18 husky and weighed 165 pounds. I'm only five-foot-one as a grown-ass woman. Words can hurt along with sticks, stones, and jeers. Why do fat kids need the word husky attached to their clothes? Isn't that double jeopardy?

Sandy's in prison. Sheila has been a few times by now also. My childhood was truly one of a kind. I should take a poll to see how many grew up hearing, "You have a collect call from…."

6

Aaron and Lillie were in good health despite being septua- and sexagenarians. Sometimes though Aaron had issues with urinating. Looking back, I'm sure he had prostate issues though he never complained. I never saw him in pain or any way other than himself.

Lillie didn't drive. I think that was common back then. Aaron had to drive himself about 45 minutes away in the middle of the night so that he could be catheterized. I never have been and hope to God that I never will be. I know that's gotta hurt.

I had to go to the pediatrician once because I couldn't pee. I remember the doctor making me drink a lot of dark soda. I'm pretty sure that I had a UTI and worms. I ate stuff out of the garden that wasn't properly washed. Worms look weird, more so when they're coming out of you. I don't drink sodas anymore or eat things that are not properly washed. Lesson learned.

Ms. Elledge was my fifth-grade teacher. Her daughter Melinda had been in most of my classes. She was smart and had a good family. What I remember about Melinda was that she could recite the books of the Bible forwards and backwards. That was impressive at any age.

My weight had begun to go down a little. I had a denim skirt with a zipper in the front. It was a 13/14. I think boys were beginning to notice me, but I was not ready to notice them. Keith Watkins touched my butt and I hit him so hard with my lunch box that the box flew across the floor with the handle still in my hand. Sorry about that, Keith.

That may've triggered a string of new looks from the opposite sex. Maybe I should enjoy this new attention.

This may cause a stir, but oh well…the guy who played the piano at church played with me also. Uh huh. I pretended to be upstairs while he practiced while everyone else was downstairs in the basement. Yep, the ivories weren't all that Chucky was playing with.

With all of this attention came a war of my wardrobe. A light switch went off in my head telling me that I was covered up too much. Lillie and I were at constant battle about my clothes. Why should she care? She didn't have to wear it.

7

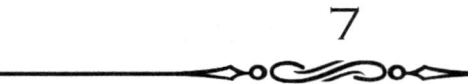

I caught the attention of two boys up the road. Mark and I rode the bus and he was a grade ahead of me in school. He wasn't that cute, but his friend was. I hope that Mark grew into his ears. Mark's friend was Dink, the cutest white boy I've ever seen, and he had 3rd Bass, a rap group, shaved into the back of his head. And he was on the wrestling team. He could wrestle me any day. I guess I was Sally Super Slut at 13. I called it a threesome, others may call it a train. Either way, YOLO!

Mark and Dink rode their bikes down to my house in the middle of the night. I'd sneak them in, fuck, and go to school the next day as if nothing had ever happened. Damn, I was slick.

Around the age of 14 I'd had my eyes set on Curtis, one of Mark's friends, who'd recently moved from Ohio. Curtis and I had the same birthday. That was cool. I guess you can say that he was my first boyfriend. We snuck around on the days that Lillie worked. Sheila was supposed to be my babysitter. We know how well that went. Aaron embarrassed me once when Curtis came over. He announced that Blue was here to see me. Curtis was dark skinned. Everyone thought that I preferred lighter-skinned people.

I shut that stigma down with Curtis. I just like people. Curtis and I attended my eighth-grade prom. He was good people, but we fizzled out after eight months. Why? Because Curtis didn't believe in oral sex. Ha! He had to go.

8

My eating habits changed along with my attire. I moved around a lot with the help of Denise Austin and a few others that I saw on TV. I developed a love for exercise that I still have today. I am a personal trainer among other things now. Things are beginning to relax a little for me now. I even gain a little freedom. Lillie allows me to go to the movies and mall with Sheila. I'm catching eyes and Sheila's catching charges. Aren't we a fine match?

I read about a summer job in the newspaper and pitched my idea to Lillie and Aaron. Aaron always let Lillie make the decisions, i.e. sign the report cards, etc. Believe it or not, it didn't take as much goading as I'd expected. Aaron drove me to and fro. It was great! I used to think watching the news was lame and boring. Well, I guess I've made it to Oldville 'cause I'll cuss you out if you interrupt my news now.

The job was at my soon-to-be senior high school. I was excited to make some money, gain some independence, and maybe expand my social skills. I befriended a boy named Jamie. He was about my height and wouldn't grow taller because he had dived off a shallow pier and cracked his skull. He had a soft spot in his head like a baby.

Creepy.

I also befriended a red-headed girl named April. We exchanged numbers and spoke frequently. I had purchased a cordless phone from Radio Shack. I thought that I was the shit because I had actually bought this phone. The outlet was in my grandparents' room, but it was my phone. I received a government monthly check. Lillie and Aaron gave me a portion. It was never uncommon even at an early age for me to have money. I proved to be more responsible than Sheila, and I could be trusted. I'd had my own savings account at the bank since fourth grade. I loved depositing money and only withdrew on holidays when I made major purchases.

I knew how to endorse checks, balance checkbooks, and to appreciate the hard-earned dollar. How could Sheila have not obtained the same skills that were shown to her?

The phone was my best friend. I had more of a phone life than a physical life. I was more scholastic growing up. I entered and won several essay and oratorical contents. My intellectual cattiness became an asset. I was never afraid of public speaking, probably because I craved the attention.

Lillie was always running me off the phone. Ugh! Leave me alone. I'm 14 now. At some point I'm gonna grow up, leave the nest, and be out of your hair. I wish that would be sooner than later.

We left work early one day and called our rides. April's ex-brother-in-law was her ride. I guess because I had been so socially deprived, I thought the concept of a brother-in-law at that age was so neat. April's ride spoke to me over the phone. He introduced himself as C.L. and told me to meet him at his car the following morning. I had not noticed him before, but apparently, he had noticed me.

C.L. surprised me with a single yellow rose, which is a symbol of friendship. C.L. had curly hair, cut-off shorts, and a thin mustache. He wasn't dressed to impress on the first impression, but I found his gesture to be genuine, sweet, and I thought that he was kinda cute. All of this would've been fine except for the fact that I was 14 and C.L. was 29.

9

I felt really connected to C.L. despite the age difference. I was also alone because I couldn't divulge my relationship to anyone. Eventually I began to mention certain aspects of C.L., omitting the age difference, of course.

Mary is someone I still spoke to from elementary school. I had introduced her and her now-husband. I remember once when they came to the house Lillie made them leave because Mary sat on Marty's lap. That's so crazy. We were all just kids. You know this shit with C.L. would never fly if she blew a gasket about that.

There was only one person that knew about C.L.—Sheila. You're probably thinking, "WTF?" but Sheila was on drugs. She went along with whatever paid the bills. Sheila would sign me out from school while C.L. waited in the car. We would take her to various stores to boost and give her a little "hush mouth" money. Things seemed to work out well that way.

I think that it was only fair that she covered for me. When she would come in drunk and high in the middle of the night, I got up to let her in and clean up her messes. I lied to Lillie and Aaron, saying that she was in before dawn. She attempted to be respectful of her parents' rules even though she was an adult. Of course, good old April was always around to smooth things over.

My entire ninth grade year consisted of checking in at homeroom, collecting my assignments, and sneaking off once a week. I remained on the honor roll and made sure that I returned in time to catch the bus ride home. I must pat myself on the back and say that I never got caught. I would've been D.O.A. if I'd have gotten caught.

10

Sometimes C.L. and I would go to the movies. My grandfather didn't like to drive after dark, and Sheila could not be trusted to use the car. Aaron dropped me and Sheila off and a "cousin" was supposed to drive us home. He was paid off and away we went with C.L. At some point we hooked her up with a guy that C.L. worked with who had a van with a bed in the back. His name was "Dr. Love." I have no idea why because he was the ugliest motherfucker I've ever seen. Rumor had it that his dick was 10 inches. I'll never know. After a few drinks he and Sheila began to cozy up. I'm positive that she never slept with him, but he constantly tried to date her after that. I guess even Sheila has standards. Well, kind of.

Let me tell you about Bobby. He was one of Sheila's boyfriends who seemed to be on the right track. He worked two jobs and worshipped the ground that Sheila walked on. Of course, that was foreign to her. She went to prison a couple of times while dating Bobby. He stuck it out for about five years. He finally reached his limit and ended it. I never saw her give a damn before. She stalked Bobby. We would "happen" to visit the store he worked, and she would have me talk to him in hopes to win him over for her. If she would've known this, I wonder how her tune would've changed.

Sheila was such a procrastinator. It took her forever to get ready to go somewhere. I ran up the steps of their apartment to rally her down only thinking that I would be there a sec. Bobby came on to me and put his hand up my shirt while standing behind me. What we didn't notice was that Lillie had popped her head in. I had left the door ajar. Oh, shit. She cussed him and threatened that if it ever occurred again, she would tell my grandfather who owned several guns. It didn't happen again. Sheila nor Aaron ever found out.

11

The rural town seemed to shrink as the whispers grew. I played dumb when Lillie questioned me. I hated to deny the person that I was in love with, but I had to protect him. We had a perfect life planned. Our song was "(Everything I Do) I Do It for You" by Bryan Adams. We were careful to keep our relationship a secret until C.L. showed up at school one day and got chased off by the principal. There was also an incident where Lillie had to pick me up from school and C.L.'s name had been on the sign-out sheet. I lied and said that he was trying to see me, but they wouldn't let him. My periods were rough, and I'd often have to miss at least one day a month for school.

I love taking pictures. I love taking them of others, but I am not camera shy on the flipside of that. A neighbor of C.L.'s took a picture of us that I found absolutely gorgeous. He wasn't one to ever show a full smile. I also captured a playful side where I sprayed Cool Whip on his dick and snapped a picture.

C.L. and his ex-wife were legally separated when we met. They lived together but worked opposite shifts to eliminate a babysitter. I loved his kids who were at least 10 years younger than me. I began to think of them as my own. I was not fond of his ex nor was she a fan of me. I did not like her negligence as a mother. I was very advanced for my age and felt as though I had my life in order.

12

Sheila began to be a turncoat. If C.L. and I didn't cater to her wishes, she'd drop hints to Lillie about C.L. and I. Sheila and I were never close, so why was I not surprised by this? Lillie was my Ma, but she began to turn on me too. It was her way of protecting me, but all I saw was punishment. I was naïve and in love.

Aaron always watched me at a distance. I know that he would've moved heaven and earth for my safety. Aaron never once said the words, "I love you," but his actions from beginning to end proved otherwise. Aaron asked me only once if I was messing around. "Boy, you ain't messing with that man, are you?" I uttered the one-word answer of, "No." Damn. Aaron could've fixed this if I'd have only known what awaited me.

Lillie became more tyrannical by the day. She checked my pads to see how many had been used and rambled through my drawers. Ugh! I'm 15 and a freshman in senior high. Where's my privacy?

Although I had not gone to the doctor, I was pregnant. I knew the instant that I became that way. I was going to finish school, the neighbor was going to babysit, and everything was going great.

C.L. and I would have a happy, loving, blended family, unlike the one that I had. My baby would always know that it was loved and wanted. My baby would never grow up hearing the words, "I'd never have another kid the sun shined on." Emotional scars are often irreversible and often irreparable.

13

I was pregnant and I indeed knew stress was not good for the baby. All I wanted was to be left alone. At some point I even thought of breaking up with C.L. I wasn't allowed to be happy and that was unfair to me. C.L. and I were in a good place. Due to Sheila's capriciousness, the reins were kept extremely tight on me. Sheila was just a wild child. They always bailed her out. If they had exuded some tough love, perhaps she would've viewed life differentially and appreciated the good life that she had. Sheila had a permanent safety net, yet no one was willing to throw me a lifeline. I had no sense of support or security except C.L.

My life was unbearable at times. I hated to get off the school bus because I lived in a war zone. Just when I thought that my life couldn't get any worse, Lillie mentioned the unthinkable. She gave me the ultimatum of having C.L. arrested for statutory rape or force me to have an abortion. What? How is it possible to hate someone that you don't know? Why would you force me to kill mine when you forced Sheila to keep me? Growing up knowing and being told that you were unwanted is a personal torture.

Lillie and Aaron were black and although they associated with those outside of their race, C.L.'s color played a major role of the unwantedness of my baby. I've never seen color as a factor of love. I view individuals just as they are.

So, now what? What am I supposed to do now? I could not fathom my life without C.L. or this baby. I packed a bag and left it on the back porch. Aaron found it. Maybe we can do something drastic and that'll bring us closer together like you see on TV. Everyone will forget the bad and focus on each other, right?

14

C.L. had brought over a jug of gasoline. On September 4th after one of my more combative days I poured gasoline in my house and lit the lighter. In my 15-year-old theoretical mind, the plan sounded great. Once I saw the flames, I had an "Oh shit!" moment and attempted to call the fire department on the cordless phone that I was holding.

I was on the phone with C.L. while I set the fire. He was no more than a 10-minute drive away. Why wasn't he present? Hell, he had all of these bright ideas, why didn't he do it himself?

The fire had consumed the phone line and I ran to the neighbor's house for help. My life was unraveling before my very eyes. What the fuck have I just done?

The fire department came quickly and assessed my grandmother who was outside in the yard. Aaron had succumbed to his death by smoke inhalation. Some visuals are hard to erase.

Everyone began to look at me with suspicion. I was told that I was treated for shock at the hospital, but to this day I do not recall. Aaron's sister, aunt Emily, and Sheila were at the hospital. I wanted to go with C.L. but Aunt Emily wouldn't allow it. I was clad in my favorite shortie PJs and some cheap slide-on Kmart shoes.

15

The silence at my aunt's house is deafening. Sheila has the nerve to stare at me angrily. I'm balled up on the couch, hugging my knees. Now would've been the time for her maternal skills to kick in.

A detective and S.B.I. agent appeared and began a barrage of questions. They questioned me in the dining room with neither of the adults present. Surely, you're not surprised by this. I am 15, alone, pregnant, and afraid. Is anyone on my side? Does anyone care? I speak few words and they only consist of "I don't knows." What am I supposed to say? I am fucked up and I have fucked up.

The deputy decides to take me in for more questioning. I am cuffed and driven away. No one has uttered a word for my rescue. Everyone hates me and they don't even know why. I comply, thinking that I'll be released. I've only known how the law works vicariously through Sheila and Sandy. I have no first-hand knowledge. I said that I wouldn't run after I was cuffed. I don't think that he was willing to take any chances.

Where was C.L.? What has he said? How could this have happened? My baby that no one knew that I was carrying…my

God, what have I done?

The police are very tricky bastards. You hear this a lot, but I've lived it. They had the nerve to tell me that they were my friends and that their perception of me wouldn't change.

I definitely did not have the right people in my life growing up which didn't expose me to people who had my best interests at heart. My body was grown but my brain was of a child. I was so socially inadequate…I wonder how many of the grown men that hit on me saw that?

I had to figure life out on my own and obviously I had not done a good job thus far. At some point the police became frustrated with me and said that if I didn't tell them how the fire began they'd bring in an arson specialist who would. After about 17 hours of their grilling me, I admitted that I did it.

From what I was told, C.L. cracked under pressure first. I guess we know who the weaker sex is. I still believed that if I told them what they wanted that I'd be released. I'm still awaiting that moment.

I was painted as this young slut who had this man under her spell. Would you believe that a psychiatrist who evaluated C.L. said that he had a tendency to do what the women in his life wanted him to? Are you fucking serious? I'm fif-fucking-teen!

16

I was appointed a guardian ad litem and criminal attorney. I'm up shit creek without a paddle. A guardian ad litem represents minors. It isn't like any other adult in my life gave a damn.

The criminal attorney had a reputation of being the best. He's now a district court judge. Too bad that my crime wasn't a traffic ticket.

I was housed initially in a juvenile facility but had to be moved to Raleigh in safekeeping due to my condition. Safekeeping is for those who are pretrial with medical conditions, snitches, or some high-profile case.

I arrived at about 11 o'clock p.m. Prison is like Motel 6, they leave the light on for you. I was greeted by some old, big, black woman. Greeted just means that she checked me in. There were no smiles, bells, or whistles. Checking my belongings didn't take long. I only had a couple of pieces of jewelry and some papers.

For some reason hiding in the clothes racks came to mind. I used to do that when I was little. I was just being a brat. I'd tell Lillie that maybe someone would find me and treat me better. I'm still on the hunt for "better." There are so many days that I wish I could've remained hidden.

Every orifice you possess is checked when you enter prison. You are stripped naked even down to your dentures if you have them, and if you think your tampon is safe, think again. If your breasts sag, you'll lift them. You will spread your ass cheeks and pussy like a cheap whore with every single search, no questions asked. Once you're degraded and deloused, you are assigned to your new residence from hell.

17

I was very young and very pregnant, so I was locked in an isolation room in the back of the infirmary. I had limited communication except for an occasional nurse and my unborn baby. Communication with safekeepers is prohibited.

I was allowed an hour of recreation outside in a small yard. I walked around and enjoyed the fresh air. While I was in my room I did push-ups, sit-ups, and yoga.

I read everything they brought me while trying to make sense of what was going on. I was allowed to use the phone but the only people that I had to call were Marie, C.L.'s mom, and my stepmother, Elvetha. Both were a godsend. Marie never blamed me for C.L.'s troubles and looked forward to her new grandchild.

Your calls are collect. There are so many that turn their backs on people once they're locked away. Your friends and often your family become only memories. Marie sent me $20-25 a month and I called her once a week. At least I had someone on the outside.

Prison can be like a maze. You know that there's a way out, but you just don't know which way to go.

I received letters from C.L. Inmates could correspond then, it is now prohibited except for approved situations. Your case was blasted across TV and that would often bring an influx of mail. You'd be surprised at how nosy society can be where criminals are concerned. If you were fortunate, someone would write of genuine concern. Most were hack jobs who had more issues than you.

I met a lady named Emily who cleaned the infirmary. We would sneak a conversation here and there. I also met a woman named Blackie who was also pregnant.

18

My attorney visited only once before I gave birth. He said that it was too far of a travel to consult with me. He protested against me going but obviously he lost.

Inmates are moved to a double room two weeks before they give birth. I shared a room with an older white lady who had heart problems. On Sunday morning I couldn't sit still. I walked up and down the hall walking out what I thought was gas. It was my first pregnancy, so I believed the midwife knew what she was talking about when she told me that I was due on the 25th. I'd had Braxton Hicks in the past and didn't want to be embarrassed by thinking that I was in labor again.

My roommate said, "Honey, I think your gas is getting kinda regular." I did not want to have to go to the hospital all shackled and looking crazy but when the nurse assessed me, my contractions were five minutes apart.

There are only a handful of staff that are sympathetic to inmates. Most are power driven, spiteful, and truly think that they're above the law.

Let me tell you a story about one in particular who was one

of the nastiest bitches you'll ever meet. She was a hood-rat who'd probably never had a full-time job prior to being a correctional officer. Her son got arrested for raping an underage white girl. She returned to work when her son's ordeal was over. He received a life sentence, by the way. The bad part is that the chip on her shoulder increased to a boulder. I hope that karma does not return to bite her son in the ass.

There were two officers that were cool, Ms. Lawrence, a thin, black woman, and Ms. Dunn, a blond who probably listened to R&B when no one was around. I always teased them by saying that I was gonna wait until they worked to have my baby. When a trip was announced, Ms. Dunn could do nothing but laugh.

You are still handcuffed and shackled in labor. Your silver never leaves you until you leave. I don't wear any jewelry except for a watch now. I feel a little constricted by it, like shackles and chains.

My "gas" was in full effect. My dumb ass is still not convinced that I'm in labor. I'm only 16 and I really believe that I'm supposed to give birth on April 25th. It's only April 19th, they're just gonna send me back. Right?

Hospital halls are so long but I'm a soldier. "Do you need a wheelchair?"

"No, I've got it."

"Oooh…" I bow over.

"Ma'am, are you alright?"

"Whew. I'm good."

Man, where is this birthing room?

"Oooh…"

"Ma'am, are you sure that you're alright?"

"Whew, this gas is killing me."

I trudge along for what seems like an eternity and get on the labor bed. My contractions are now three minutes apart. Okay. I'm convinced. I feel it now. I tested positive for group B strep in my eighth month so I must have an IV with penicillin. I still hate needles. I cannot, however, have anything for pain because the baby would be born sleepy. Okay, I've got this.

I'm 16, giving birth under armed guards. Regardless of how nice they are, let me try to run and they'll shoot me dead. Don't ever forget that.

My labor isn't long. I'm too stubborn to scream. My periods hurt worse than my labor, so I was okay. Two-and-a-half hours later I gave birth on Easter Sunday morning to a 7-pound five-ounce boy. I'd had a couple of names picked out, but I settled on Colt. It's a strong Native name. It really fit him. Wow, I did it.

19

After Colt was taken to be checked, etc. Ms. Dunn asked if I'd looked in the mirror. No, I just shit out an elephant. She handed me a mirror and let me tell you something…I was fucked up. Aside from my pregnancy not being sexy because I did not scream, the pressure came out in my face. I broke every blood vessel in my face and eyes. My face resembled a road map.

Later that day when Colt was brought back, he was so beautiful. He was such an angel until he cried. What in the hell? He had a scream that belonged in a haunted house. Oh my God…he hated me. I was afraid of him. I tried to console him but ended up crying more than him. The next set of officers and nurses calmed him and me too. Yikes.

Colt wasn't one of those wobbly-headed babies. Maybe it was because of all of that damn milk that I drank and my vegetarian lifestyle. I had a little heartburn and a little swelling. That was probably due to my 47-pound weight gain. I returned to my normal 120 pounds within six weeks. Too bad that I cannot return there now.

Karen was the only one of Sheila's friends who didn't get into trouble. I'd known her all of my life. She had a son that was my age, so she wasn't a stranger. She also had biracial children, two sets of twin girls, so I thought that he would fit in.

I spent two days with Colt. How can a mother give up their children? Giving Colt to my friend was by far the hardest thing I've ever done. I fought so hard for him to live. Despite of or along with the lives that I took, my life left when I handed him over to Karen.

As you read these words, imagine the pain that I felt and still feel. The world portrays me as a monster. All I ever wanted to be seen as was a mother.

20

I returned to prison feeling empty and broken. I was fortunate enough to still be in my room alone which gave me much-needed time to heal mentally and physically. Once I was medically cleared, I was moved to an area that should've been condemned. I've seen tent shelters on TV that looked more habitable.

The cell had four bunks and lots of bars. There was a ceramic bowl on bricks that resembled half of a chimney for the toilet. What in the fuck was this? We had put a makeshift clothesline from one end of the top bunks to the other with a sheet in front of it for privacy. If the people who slept on top were on their bunks you could still be seen. Privacy is the first thing you lose in prison. The living conditions were less than desirable, to say the least. For the most part people were just trying to make it until they went to court.

Dorm C is what it was called. It was a very run-down building infested with roaches and something called water bugs that were territorial. One flew--yes, they flew--and landed on my hair. Ugh!! I almost died.

There was only one other person in my cell. She was a young girl who was also facing murder charges. There must've been something in the water. I'm not a social butterfly and I stay in my space. I can live with pretty much anyone, and believe you me, I have. Society has the misconception that most people in prison are drug addicts, are from poor backgrounds, and are uneducated. I can assure you that the inmates on average were more established than the staff, which is why a lot of staff are intimidated and abuse their authority over us.

Blackie was a familiar face in safekeeping. I assumed that she gained that nickname because she had black hair. It was, in fact, due to the black eyes that she used to sport. Blackie was, like 80 percent of the other women in prison, involved with the wrong guy. Some even take the blame believing that he will "hold you down." The only thing that he's done so far is hold you back.

Blackie gave birth about two months before me and was only a couple of years older. I think that her motherly instincts kicked it early because she adopted me as her "state daughter." Women are natural nurturers and form bonds rather quickly. State families, i.e., moms, dads, brothers, sisters, etc., are very common in prison and often continue once released.

Blackie had a small circle of friends, two of them were Connie and Dana. They were a couple but not codefendants. Lesbians have never been a big deal to me. I'm okay with who I am and who I love. I remember reading a Hustler magazine when I was young and calling the 1-800 phone number.

I ran the phone bill up to $300. When Lillie asked if I made those calls, I lied. This was around age 10 or 11. I blamed the phone bill on Sheila. I was 14 when I finally confessed that it was me.

I also had a neighbor named Robin whom I thought was beautiful. She had the bluest eyes and biggest boobs. Robin also had a baby at 14.

My sixth and ninth grade teachers were gay. I could tell back then. I also had a couple of male cousins that I was exposed to as a child.

My diverse upbringing and exposure to a variety of people have made my life, especially in prison, easier. I didn't realize how closed-minded people could be. Perhaps that's one of the catalysts for their unhappiness.

21

I endured safekeeping for 334 days. My attorney only visited me once after my transfer to Raleigh. It shouldn't have mattered that the drive was three-plus hours away. Wasn't his job to offer me the best defense possible?

My initial charges sounded like I was the Unabomber. I had a charge for malicious use of an explosive incendiary device, malice aforethought, premeditation, first degree arson, conspiracy to commit murder, and two counts of first-degree murder.

I was labeled as a monster and given far more power than I possessed. If I were that powerful, wouldn't I have convinced C.L. to commit the crime and take the charges?

I signed a plea bargain 106 days after giving birth. I pled guilty to two counts of first-degree murder, the remaining charges were dismissed.

On August 2nd I returned to the wonderful Wilkes County jail. Even though I had signed a plea bargain, I had something that resembled a trial. Character witnesses on my behalf and for the State were present. How much of a character could a now-16-year-old have?

On my behalf was Elvetha who spoke of my troubled childhood and how she tried to fill in the gaps of my lack of parental guidance.

Sherry was the one who was going to be our babysitter. The D.A. tried to discredit her, painting her to be a "hoochie mama."

Mary, the one who Lillie ran off from the house, spoke of my sometimes-physical abuse such as belt welts and the verbal abuse that she'd observed.

Ms. Chapman was my music teacher who spoke highly of me. She talked about how I helped doing bulletin boards and getting her classroom ready for the upcoming school year.

22

The D.A. had a totally different band of characters. Aaron's nephew said that I was spoiled, received everything that I wanted, and said that Aaron would be buying me a car when I turned 16. Why in the hell didn't I know of any of this?

Oh…and there was my godmother. This old bat said that I was an ungrateful, unappreciative child. She recalled buying me a gift when I was 10 and how I acted out. She didn't recall the gift, but I did. She bought me a red plaid set of dishrags. Unless I specifically asked for dishrags as a housewarming gift, I would not appreciate dishrags as a grown-ass woman, would you? So, forgive me for not wanting to be ecstatic about being Molly Maid.

The D.A. said that this was not Burger King and that I shouldn't have it my way by receiving a two-for-one deal. I hear that he died in a hunting accident. They say that if you don't have anything nice to say, don't say anything at all. He's dead? Good. I guess I'm still working on that part of my forgiveness journey.

My attorney said that one-life terms would be a significant amount of time, blah, blah, blah. The deliberation took two days. On August 2nd, 1992, I rose before Judge Beaty to receive my punishment which one life after the exploration of life. I must serve a 40-year minimum before I'm eligible or even considered for parole. I will be 55 years old. Everyone received a death sentence after this ordeal.

23

I returned to Raleigh but in a slightly different section from safekeeping. You must do what's called adjustment time once you receive a lengthy sentence. It was 60 days back then. I think it's omitted now, it's a waste of time. Being sentenced to forever and having silence to dwell on that is not what is needed. Support and to see those who have gotten past where you are is a much better tool for survival and success.

Speaking of survival, what in the hell was I gonna do now? My attorney could not spare me from prison, but he did give me money out of his wallet. He and his secretary gave me $50 to bring with me. Is that what my life is worth? That was a selfless gesture. I really appreciated that.

So much is going on in my mind. What's gonna happen to C.L.? When will I see Colt? After I received my sentence, I received 110 letters, mostly from other inmates. I barely get two letters now. Where are all of my adoring fans?

One of the people who wrote was a guy on death row who maintained his innocence. We wrote for about 15 years before they executed him. I wonder if DNA could've reversed his death sentence. I miss Sammy.

I received a couple of letters from people who were not incarcerated, thank God. Orlando began to visit, send money, care packages, etc. He looked out for a long time, and he was really cool. I wish that I could repay or at least show my gratitude for those who've helped me along the way. God knows they've all showed up when I needed someone.

24

During my adjustment I met an Amazon named Tonya. She was like six-feet-one-and-a-half inches, about 220 pounds. Compared to my five-foot frame she made me look tiny. Tonya was funny, could sing, and bought everything she thought that I would like. Tonya tried her damnedest to get me to like her, but I just wasn't feelin' her. I had enough shit on my mind without involving somebody else.

I'd been talking to Tonya for a few months, so I knew a lot about her. Tonya came to my cell visibly upset and shaken because her grandfather, whom she was close to, died in a head-on crash. She told me through sobs that she loved me and that I was always mean to her. To this day I have no idea where this rebuttal came from. I told her that I was sorry and that I loved her too. What? Where'd that come from? It's amazing how a tragedy can bring people together no matter how hard you attempt to suppress your feelings.

After my adjustment time was up, I went to what's called regular population. Tonya remained in Dorm C while awaiting trial. It was against the rules to communicate, but I snuck by every day to see her.

On population you have access to small doses of everything that you can get when you're free, both legal and illegal. You also have the typical B.S. rules that go along with prison. As long as you don't blatantly break the rules in the staff's face, a blind eye is often turned.

There's weed, cigarettes, sex with both staff and inmates. It's like a flea market with lots of bartering and trading. If you run short of cash, you can visit the loan shark for a two-for-one deal. When you borrow a noodle or dollar the unspoken rule is that you pay two back. If you don't, you can expect some consequences, sometimes when you least expect them.

25

Some people you can look at and know to avoid. Others you'll forge a bond that'll last a lifetime. It's best to find your own routine and always keep your eye on the prize (freedom).

You'll be assigned a case manager who'll help you with classes and a job. Inmates do not sit around all day as you may think. Prison is not a resort, it's the worst mental hospital that you'll ever visit. You're under constant scrutiny, ignored, and attempted to feel less than human.

This works for the weaklings who lack discipline and self-esteem. For the motherfuckers like me who know who they are it poses a problem when you hit them with their own kiss-my-ass attitude. Oh well...

I'm assigned to G.E.D. which is cool with me. I've always liked school and it's a requirement to take college classes. I entered G.E.D. in October and by that December I had completed and passed all classes. When you have no one to rely on but yourself, one of two things will occur—you'll succeed or fail. You'd be surprised at how often they happen simultaneously.

26

The prison compound is 13.5 acres, and everything is in a separate building. You must walk everywhere you go such as meals, work, school, etc. accompanied with a walking pass.

They have a gym which I frequent when I'm not walking laps and sneaking to talk to Tonya.

The shoes that are given when entering prison should be illegal. They have no support and no traction. And because you must walk through snow, hail, and rain, they get holey really quickly. You can only get a pair every 90 days. My friend Mary nicknamed them SSKs (slip, slide, and kill a nigga). Damn, I hated those shoes. The ones that were sold weren't much better. You'll only get an irregular, no-name brand of whatever the Bob Barker state brand is. No, it isn't the "Price Is Right" Bob Barker.

You could have clothes, shoes, and other items sent in when I came to prison. The state thought that it was cost effective for them to furnish our clothes. You should see us now looking like clones in clown clothes.

The building that I lived in first had a semi-private room, two to a room with a door. As long as you get along with your roommate in your four-by-four room, it's okay. The walls begin to shrink and so does your patience.

My first roommate was an old crotchety bitch who'd been down forever. She had so much shit in the room that it looked small. I hope that I didn't turn into that lady.

I know that my age had a lot to do with my defiance but if I'm sentenced as an adult, when will I be treated as one?

27

I become friends with Mary. She's older, dark-skinned, does crossword puzzles, and talks the most shit. Mary's health failed and she became dependent upon dialysis. She has been released but I wonder if she's even alive.

Dreamer is one of the most beautiful older white women that I've seen. She has silver hair and a very young spirit. She becomes my friend, a mother friend, and a good ally. Dreamer was released after two hip replacements, one that the state fucked up and 33 years later.

Trina was angelic, sweet, and kind. She did a lot of needlepoint. Beautiful things. Trina had a boyfriend who told her about his crime after he'd committed it. She assumed that he was drunk and out of his mind until the police kicked her door in looking for him and wondering why she didn't report him. Trina is out also but only because an attorney found a discrepancy and she was granted an M.A.R.

All of these people were closer to me than the one who birthed me. I had some rough patches and I'm so grateful to have had them to lean on.

You are pulled in so many places when you're young. I'm only 16 and that creates challenges of its own. You don't realize that the adults in your life want the best for you because at that age you don't know what that best is. I thought I did.

Tonya finally got her time and made it to the compound. She was sentenced to seven years. Relationships of a sexual nature are frowned upon in prison, even still in the world even though they are now legal.

If there is a crack or crevice to sneak a kiss, have sex, or make some other deal, we'll find it. I enjoy being with Tonya. Our relationship blossomed organically and was rather solid.

As wonderful as she was, Tonya had a habit. She liked to gamble and drink hooch. Hooch is prison-made wine. It stinks to high heaven to me but many drink it. I don't think it'll ever go out of fashion.

I got money from Marie. Tonya got a little money and I always budgeted. When she won, she won. But when she lost...ugh! Mary taught me to crochet which became a profitable side business for me.

Inmates and staff paid good money for crocheted items such as clothes, blankets, and toys for themselves or for their loved ones. We had cash then. A dollar went a long way. I never smoked but I remember that cigarettes were 60 cents a pack for the cheap ones. There was a limit as to how much we could possess weekly—it was $30. Anything in excess (if found) was considered contraband. I was fortunate that it was never found.

28

Back in the day inmates could wear their own clothes. The only state-issued clothing you wore was a shirt or dress, the color was indicative of the custody level. I was and still am rather shapely. I have ample boobs, small waist, and above average gluteus maximus. My hair is usually shoulder length or longer and my attitude stays on check. I gather the attention of both males and females. Variety is the spice of life. I'm rarely interested in one person. It's not that I'm whorish, even though at times I am. I just like different aspects of different people.

There's constant interaction with outsiders whether it be staff or visitors. We had male inmate maintenance workers who roamed around the compound. Most of them had a cool supervisor who was down with whatever. Prison was a world of fun back then. I bet you're wondering if I partook…well, hell yeah, I did. I had a dark-skinned fella that dropped money, letters, and pictures at certain spots. We had a few "moments" but nothing extreme.

There was one (fast forward) that I pumped the brakes on. I met him at "the spot" just knowing that he'd back out. Nah, it was me. I'm so bad to call someone's bluff. I can't believe that someone called mine. He was one of the first of many staff that I was involved with.

Women get a lot of visitors. Many of us are mothers before anything else and do all that we can to connect to our children and those who matter to us in general.

Some women have been known to fudge a few things too. Sugar daddies are (usually) older men who dote on attractive women. They visit, send money and packages, and it gives you someone to call. Orlando is my friend. I guess you could also say my boyfriend. And if you want to be ratchet you can say sugar daddy.

I have a double-life sentence and a girlfriend who gambles way too much. Someone must pay the bills around here. As hard as I work to do what's necessary, would you believe that Tonya cops an attitude periodically? The nerve.

I'm almost 18 and I'm trying to get my life in some sort of semblance of order. I think that I'm doing better than most until Sheila comes to prison.

29

Yeah, that's what the hell I said. My grandparents' funeral was delayed for over a week because Sheila got ghost. Who knows where she went, but do you know that some thought that I was covering for her? There's no way in hell that I would've done that.

Anyway, I hadn't heard from her since the crime and here she comes. Drugs apparently affect your memory because she acted as though I was the best thing since sliced bread and that I'm the apple of her eye.

As time evolved, I disclosed my past to my friends and Tonya. They knew the real deal about Sheila before she exuded her phony ways which were very transparent to all.

She only had a few months. I just wanted to limit my interaction and get through it. Sheila didn't prepare for her entry to prison. How could she when I had removed her safety net? Sheila wanted to be introduced to my friends who were mostly her age or older. Sheila wanted to meet Orlando and know in-depth details. Sheila also wanted me to take care of her materially because I appeared to be straight. We've had food sales, canteen, etc. She wouldn't relent until I gave in. I gave way more than I should've in all aspects. Was she appreciative? No. She would bring up the past when she didn't get her way.

The compound may've been several acres but news, especially bad news, travels fast. I had random people walk past me and say shit like, "I can't believe that you talk to your mother that way." I can honestly say that when my friends caught wind of such, they diffused the situation before I could say a word. Those are real friends.

Sheila's few months came and went ending with promises to write, visit, have a number so that I could call her, etc. Those words went in one ear and out of the other.

30

Women are far sneakier than men. I had to remind you of that. Tonya and I have been together for two years now. Things are becoming unsettled. In layman's terms, the bitch been cheatin'. It came out of left field too. I questioned her about it. Of course, it was nothing. "I won't do it again." You've heard that before, right?

The chick's name was Shirley who also played cards. She was busted. I mean dusty and homely. She didn't even qualify as a butta girl—everything looked good but her face. No. She was a BMW—Body Made Wrong. I couldn't believe it. The size difference had absolutely nothing to do with me knocking Tonya upside her head. Round one.

Round two. My dumb ass believed that it was over. Tonya was chilling with Shirley behind the building. I did what every red-blooded American would do. I jumped on both of them.

Round 3. Almost 19 years old and truly at my wits' end. Yep, I went back again. I jumped on Tonya in the chicken line. When chicken is served in prison, it's a big deal. Everyone goes and the line is long. Tonya said something slick about going to eat lunch with Shirley and here I go again. A couple of people pulled me off of her then.

Sadly, enough things were just done with Tonya and I. She wasn't gonna stop cheating and I wasn't gonna stop beating. It was an adjustment, but life went on. I can't say that we ever became the best of friends because her future girlfriends were always intimidated by me. Exes are exes for a reason.

Tonya's sneaky ass also tried to intimidate my future girlfriends but when I caught word of that I set her straight. I wonder what ever happened to her.

31

Nineteen was a blah kinda year. Sheila returns again for a few months, wrecking my life. With each return trip I am stronger than before. Her bullshit blends in with everyone else's bullshit. I had limited interaction with her, and she came and went.

We have a program called WINGS that was a club. The sweetest woman in the world, Ms. Hobbs, was over it. She looked to me as her own—she never had any children. We communicated for several years after her departure. We got to wear a lot of cool costumes for various functions. I stayed with her from the time my work assignment ended until 10 p.m. when shift changed. It was as though I wasn't in prison.

A singing group performed. I got to interview them. The lead singer's name was Brian. He was cool. The band was a bunch of young boys swinging their junk around and couldn't sing. But Brian and I became close. He even got on my visitation list.

Visitation is for four hours and he came faithfully. I think that if I hadn't had this ass-load full of time, Brian and I could've worked out. Brian is one of many that did not withstand the test of time.

Realistically it would've been unfair to ask someone to put their life on hold to stick it out with me. I do not fault anyone who has come and gone out of my life, only the strong survive.

32

I've always tried to fill my days. It makes your time go by much faster when you're busy, hopefully in a productive manner.

I've taken a number of classes and had a number of jobs. Most prisons require you to work. One of my jobs was the sewing plant. Inmates make other inmate clothes among other things. It provided a steady cash flow, but factory work is not for me. I only worked there the required amount of time and got the hell away.

I took horticulture next. I absolutely loved it and loved my teacher. I loved being outside, making things grow, and learned about botanical nomenclatures. I planted two apple seeds that I stole from a Roman apple from the dining hall. We're not supposed to take anything out of the dining room, but they (the staff) rush you in and out that they leave you no choice. If you don't get money and your last meal is before 5 p.m. you're hungry and do what's necessary for survival. I guess enough of Sheila's lifestyle seeped into me because I was pretty good at pocketing things.

The funny thing about the apple seeds was that my teacher said they wouldn't grow. Slowly but surely, they began to sprout, and Johnny was born. Yeah, I named my tree after Johnny Appleseed. So what? Just for the record, Johnny still exists. Whenever I leave prison, I'm digging Johnny up and taking him with me. He's my other son and he deserves freedom also.

Every prison that I've visited feeds around the same time. Breakfast is between 6:15 and 6:45 a.m. Lunch is between 11:15 a.m. and 12:45 p.m. Dinner is between 3:45 and 4:30 p.m. After that, you're on your own.

At horticulture one day these two chicks were saying that they wished that they had a couple of bucks 'til Thursday. I ate out of the dining hall and only bought what I needed form the canteen. My money was always sporadic, so I learned to pinch pennies early. I lived with one of the known loan sharks, so I chimed in and said that I'd bring them $5 when we returned from lunch. The loan sharks had to keep their face straight for obvious reasons and had a middleman.

I brought the $5 back but secretly it was mine. We got paid on the job site. I saw who had what, so I knew they were straight. Not to pull a race card but most white girls were straight and always had money. Some gave it up really easily too. You winked at one and she was yours. Dummy. The exchange went off without a hitch and I easily turned $5 into $10. Things are looking up for me.

I still crochet and have learned a lot from those who've been crocheting awhile. I even delve into other crafts. Prison life is about survival, I cannot stress that enough. It'll never be what you want but it will be what you make of it.

33

The next girlfriend was a big Indian named Moke. Moke was cool and was full of shit. I ran up on her and her ex. I was in an unauthorized area because I didn't live there. I say, "Are you gonna be with her or me?" This weak-ass broad held her head low and pointed to the ex. Okay. Cool. I thought about that as I began to walk away and knocked her upside her head.

My friend Phaedra grabbed me and said, "Girl, let's go!" She was one of my "pull up" friends. Pull up friends save you from getting into potentially bad situations. Phaedra got out of prison, got tangled up with the wrong guy, and was accidentally killed in a drug deal gone wrong.

That's one of many stories in which people do a lot of time only to die free. I wonder sometimes…where's the free in freedom?

I have another unfortunate story while I'm on a roll. Tonya was a talented blond who had many creative talents. She did my first real prison tattoo. I did my very first, but it faded rather quickly.

Tonya served about 19 years and reconnected with her children who were babies when she came. She was out about six months riding with her son Cody. From what I'm told he reached for something and wrecked. Cody was badly injured; Tonya was killed. Can you imagine the guilt that he must carry? God rest the dead.

34

Peaches is 12 years older than me, from Trinidad, and has a sexy accent, especially when she's mad. We got along well except when my mouthiness set her off. I absolutely loved having sex with her. She's so exotic...the risk was worth the reward of being caught with her.

We were together about three years before she left. She visited me once released but returned years later. Due to her last charge, she was deported back to Trinidad. I really hate that for her. Peaches is such a good person and I hope that our paths cross again one day.

I'm doin' my thang, i.e., working and making money, when this C/O comes along. Most cringe when "Z" works because of her less than friendly persona. I remember dreading to get the blow dryer from her one day. The staff is in charge of keeping our appliances so that we won't abuse them.

I had my emerald robe on which defined my curves even more; I stood out in a crowd. Z was probably trying to flirt but I was really just trying to get the damn blow dryer. So, I didn't catch on.

On another occasion where I had to acquire a walking pass, Z asked my name. I have no idea where this came from, but I said that my name was Bubba. Of course, my cattiness made her irate. I just felt like poking the bear.

35

Z cracked on me. She turned up her flirt game saying that she could do this and that. I've never been one to back down from some words, so she was gonna have to put her mouth on her words, and hopefully me too.

I never nap. When I get up, I stay up all day, but I told Mary and a newly acquired friend named Tracey that I was laying down. It was chicken day, so the building was gonna be empty.

I had a single room and didn't have to worry about unwanted heads poppin' in. I knew that Mary and Tracey were on to my shenanigans anyway. I don't even know if this tryst is taking place but I'm gonna be ready just in case.

Well, she was all that and more. I was naked beneath my blanket then and every time she worked thereafter. For some reason, she made my clothes fall off, maybe she had a remote control.

Mary and Tracey covered for us. I really liked everything about Z. She was not as gruff as she appeared to be. She was ex-military, a mom, and she really stuck it out even when the staff caught wind of us and began giving her fucked up posts.

We broke the rules, but I appreciate everything she went through because she didn't have to.

Fast forward several years after she left--I received a letter from a male inmate who described her to a tee. She must've asked him to write a shout to me because she still worked in another facility. It felt good to know that I was thought of. I still think about her.

36

There are nice staff and assholes. One of the most precious women I've ever met was the social worker that I called Ma. She was so nurturing and loving to everyone. You can feel her aura before she comes close. Ma's presence made you calm and want to be a better person. I hope that people think of me like that one day.

I'd run errands for her like hanging up bulletins, cleaning, etc. I'd do anything to be in Ma's presence. Even if I saw her today, I'd walk through hell in gasoline drawers to get her a cup of ice water.

37

As life shows its sense of humor, Sheila returns for a third time more belligerent than ever. She's lived from pillar to post and seems angry at the world. Does that stop her from expecting a handout? Of course not.

I happened to be in lockup when she transferred to another prison. She had reached the requirement and was eligible for home passes and work release. She always seemed to receive the easy road in life. This was no different.

When I was younger, I frequented our lockup/segregation unit. I was sick of being told what to do and was very rebellious. I also felt as though my world had *my* rules and I wanted to be left alone in it. Prison felt differently.

I was fortunate enough to not see Sheila leave. What I was not fortunate enough to be spared from was the letter that she wrote. It contained typical Sheila B.S. except for the sentence, "Have a happy life—sentence, that is." How cruel and fucked up. I don't even know why it bothered me or why I remember it to this day. I did not respond and was spared several good years without her in my life.

38

Among Sheila's pitstops was a guy named David. He was nice enough to let her crash. She had mentioned me, and he became intrigued. David's mind was full of lithium and God know what other crazy meds. I do not feel like being politically correct by saying that he had mental issues. The motherfucker was bat-shit crazy!

He wanted to visit so I let him. I did not know the extent of David until visitation. He was dressed like a '60s pimp, feather plume in hate included. David received a monthly crazy check which Sheila probably pocketed. He also rocked and had the breath of a fire-breathing dragon.

What in the hell did I get myself into? Aside from that, David was nice and wanted to be helpful. I've never been one to deny free help. David looked out for a while. Look, I learned that by sitting through visitation. I still can't believe that I lived through that.

39

Angie was the next staff member that I had a tête-à-tête with, and she was a snow bunny. She came from a nice background, classy and crazy. It's always the cute ones. She was a little possessive. I know that sounds crazy, but she didn't want me talking to certain people and let it be known.

We made it work for a while and communicated for several years after she left. Angie ended up dating someone whom I'd been in prison with for quite some time. They broke up but I bet it's because Angie's craziness surfaced.

A little crazy is okay, a lot is a Lifetime movie. Angie was well on her way.

If I'm not messing around, I'm usually by myself. I've never been one to trust easily and with all of the crazy shit that I do, it's best to ride so. The small crew that I was down with was enough for me. We had eachothers' back. That's a rarity in and out of prison.

My flings are plentiful but short-lived. You only live once, right? There was something that I genuinely liked about everyone. I think that some could've lasted if I didn't have that thing called a life sentence.

Here comes a curvy Lane Bryant chick named YoYo. She's a staff but the bitch is straight. YoYo was as gorgeous as she was ditzy. Damn, I guess you can't win 'em all.

I was doing a crossword puzzle one day with the clue: burger holders, four letters. Please tell me that you didn't say hand like she did. Mary and Tracey covered for several of our "locker searches." Yeah, more sexcapades.

One of the funniest incidences that occurred in my time happened with YoYo. We were sword fighting with Christmas paper rolls and glitter when the glitter jar opened and went into my mouth. I think that I shit glitter for a whole year.

Yoyo took another job as a phlebotomist and nurse in Pennsylvania. I hope she can find the right end to take a temperature. Yikes!

40

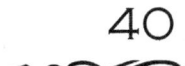

Prison can offer some positive things if you take advantage of them. MATCH (Mothers and Their Children) is a program to strengthen the bond with your child from birth to 18. You can have monthly visits in a relaxed environment that resembles an apartment. Once you attend classes you become a MATCH mom.

MATCH works best when you have a caretaker who'll cooperate. I began MATCH at age 19.

Karen had done a pretty good job of bringing Colt to see me and C.L. until C.L. died. C.L. was diagnosed with hepatitis C in 1997, by 1999 he was dead. They didn't have a cure back then and that saddens me to this day because aside of everything else, C.L. loved his son.

The chaplains kept the lines of communication open with C.L. and I during this process. It would've been equally as difficult to lose him if I were free. It's one of those things that just wasn't supposed to happen.

There was something called Family Day the day after C.L. died. Karen brought Colt and he appeared to be as good as he could. To this day he's the toughest guy that I know. I hate that life has made him be this way but he's so awesome and I'm so blessed to know him.

The next several years were very unsettling pertaining to Colt's visits. He was only eight when C.L. died. Karen moved several times and severed the lines of communication.

She hung up on MATCH and anyone else who called on my behalf. I could endure anything in life except being without Colt.

I was so distraught that I contacted Prisoners' Legal Services begging for help. They sent a paralegal to visit, investigated my claims, and decided that I had a case against Karen.

All I had to do was sign the contract to sue Karen for visitation rights. One clause stopped me from signing. "You run the risk of terminating your parental rights." If I lose, I'll never see Colt again. I wouldn't have been able to breathe if that happened.

I thought that if I'm half-ass getting to see him it's better than not at all. He was only 11 years old. I'd be damned if I'd have allowed some judge to let Colt think that I abandoned him. I'm only about 24, still trying to figure life out. I don't think that I've done such a good job of it thus far.

41

A new beau had graced my presence at this point, Shawn. She was sexy but jealous. Shawn was cool as long as she kept me secluded. You know that I'm a bit of a wildcat so that wasn't gonna last long.

A homie of mine gave me a necklace, Shawn broke it. I tried to break her neck after that. I was sitting on the porch with Mary and Tracey one day and Shawn came by popping off at the mouth. I tried to rip that bitch's tongue out of her face.

Of course, this warranted another trip to jail. I didn't give a shit. Shawn's last words were, "You ain't nothing but a project hoe." I don't know why that flew threw me, but it did and then I flew on her. Ha!

Since confession is good for the soul, I'll give you another example as to why Shawn may've been jealous. There was a sexy staff member who reminded me of Mary J. Blige. She began to flirt with me and in turn I flirted back. She wrote, "You make my panties wet" on the back of one of those walking passes, and it was on from there.

We didn't get to cross the line sexually. I would've jumped on with both feet, but she was good to look at while it lasted.

Okay, maybe Shawn was onto something. The fast forward with her is that she got a break from her time and is doing really well. We communicate still after the good, the bad, and the ugly between us. Pretty cool, huh?

42

In December of 2000, Mary and I are in school for computer information technology. Have you ever met one of these people who type at lightning speed? Mary's one of them. I'd often look at her and say, "You're making me angry [typing that fast]."

My left hand was numb. Mary saw me shaking it and asked me what was wrong. Fuck if I know. Maybe I slept on it all night or something. It was a strange feeling, like pins and needles, but eventually it subsided.

I brought in the new year by getting a little head. Isn't that how you're supposed to bring it in? On January 2, 2001 I woke up and couldn't see out of my right eye. I've heard of mind-blowing sex, but not sight-stealing sex.

I'm not a panicky person but I really couldn't see. After a day, I filled out a sick call which is usually a waste of time and money because it's not free and our medical care is shitty. My friends teased me by asking, "How many fingers do you see?" Hell. None. That's the problem.

The optician comes on Tuesdays and I saw him. He prescribed something that day, but I didn't receive it. Why?

I was immediately sent to the outside hospital the next day. I saw an ophthalmologist who prescribed steroids and some other shit. I also saw a few other specialists, one being a neurologist. I stayed gone all day.

Steroids are wonderful drugs, but they feel like gasoline being run through your veins.

I was healthy. No preexisting issues. I worked out daily and I was a vegetarian, for God's sake. I hadn't drunk, did drugs, etc., so what could've been the problem?

43

A week later I went back to the neurologist. He was a short man from Guyana with a thick accent. The doctor said that his findings were consistent with multiple sclerosis (MS).

I wasn't unfamiliar with MS because Connie and Moke had it. They were often tired and just drained looking. How could this have happened?

MS is such an iffy, scary disease. How could my life be over at 25? We discussed treatments to slow the progression of the disease. I began to research it as much as I could. I settled on an injection that's given once a week. As much as I hated needles, this one was just gonna have to work.

My crew was waiting in our sitting area outside. I didn't return until 4 p.m., I was so drained. When I broke the news, you'd have thought that they were dying right along with me. Their reaction let me know that I had chosen the right group of people to call my friends. Pam fed me crackers because steroids make you hungry and swell. Mary and her wisdom made me promise to not overdo things. Dreamer wouldn't leave my side to make sure that I didn't overdo it. Cookie, Sheila, and Tracey covered for when I did overdo it.

I've mentioned being true to myself however that may be. I didn't wallow in what my life could be and focused on the here and now. I'm still like that. I'm big on accountability, therefore I make no excuses for myself or anyone else. If you do the shit, own the shit and move past the shit.

When I went to the hospital a specific officer was chosen to go with me. I didn't know that until the ride back. I was visibly upset, crying and handcuffed, and as always alone with my thoughts.

Ms. Bullock's youngest daughter was diagnosed with MS when she was 10. She was one of the youngest cases in North Carolina. I immediately began to rethink my sadness.

She understood what I was going through more than anyone else. Ms. Bullock had other children and an older daughter who began to have symptoms of MS. The older daughter had a severe case upon diagnosis. Ms. Bullock had to leave work in order to care for her daughters. It mysteriously worked out that she drove me to all of my appointments. God does work in mysterious ways....

44

You shift around a lot in prison whether it be to another prison, dorm, or bed. You rarely stay in the same spot from the beginning to the end of your sentence. At times it's an inconvenience but it definitely keeps you on your toes.

A lot of long-termers like to live together because they like the structure and familiarity of one another. Not me. I like change of face, to see people come and go. And besides, how can you fill me in on what's going on out there if you're stuck inside with me? And I'm a bit of a troublemaker and was banished from my semi-private room. Oh well....

I live in an open quad of 34. It resembled a barracks. If you're a "private" person, so to speak, that's gone out the window quickly. I can walk around the same way that I came into the world, and it doesn't phase me. My motto is "skin is in."

I'm chillin' and checking out my new environment. You live out of a locker but the more shit that you have, the more the police can fuck with.

I also have a new job. I really like this job. I make beds and do laundry at the infirmary. There's only one chick that constantly messes her bed up. I change her sheets damn near daily, putting everything in a biohazard bag. She's disgusting and does the shit on purpose. The older people are, well…just the older people. Hell, I even help them fasten their bras or braid their hair. It doesn't cost a thing to be nice. Contrary to my belief, I may get old one day and need a smile or two myself.

While I'm at this job a guy shoots his shot. I don't entertain a lot of guys like that. I'm just usually trying to get in their pockets and not in their pants. This arrangement happened to be convenient. I go to work early—after breakfast at 6 a.m.-ish. There aren't a lot around and the residents are asleep. I didn't mind being bent over the couch a time or two. It was only a fling. The staff rotated a lot. He rotated his way out of a job because rumor had it that someone was caught sucking his dick. All I can say is that it wasn't me.

Ugh, I'm confessing again. And God knows that this one should've gone to my grave. There was a maintenance worker, a woman who started talking a little junk. Here we go again… Her teeth were jacked up, but her sex game was awesome. There were 1,000 places to screw, and we did. This was a less-than-90-days fling because she couldn't pass the required piss test. Damn, what a loser. She only had the job through nepotism anyway. How embarrassing.

45

My wonderful Ma calls for me. She probably has some memo that she wants me to pass out. Maybe she needs me to clean something. Whatever it is, I'll be mighty glad to do it.

It's June 2003, I'm 27, perhaps a little less feral. Maybe. I bounced into her office on this Tuesday to receive the surprise of my life.

Karen was sitting in Ma's office. Civilians are not allowed on the premises. This was not a visitation day. How and why was Karen here?

The room was filled with silence that made me very uneasy. Ma finally broke the silence by saying, "It's not Colt." That eased me but perplexed me just the same.

Karen produced a newspaper that read of an accident. The person who died could not be named until the next of kin was notified. The next of kin was me. Sheila had been hit and killed by a taxi while crossing the street. What?

Sheila led one of the most fast-paced lives ever. Out of everything that could've happened, why did this accident have to be her demise?

None of us could believe it. Ma allowed me to make the necessary calls and arrangements. At age 44, Sheila's life was over.

Although Sheila and I weren't close, she was a part of me. Some land from my grandparents had been discovered at some point. I had sold it to a distant relative and was living off of it. I was also saving for an attorney who could hopefully free me someday. I took part of that money and buried Sheila. She had a viewing and a casket. I don't know how her soul rests but mine rests just fine knowing that I did what I should've done for her even though she probably wouldn't have done the same for me.

I've had to let go of a lot of the hurt and hatred that I felt for her. I want the best possible relationship that I can have with Colt, and I cannot bring that mess from the past into our future.

I contacted an attorney, one of those "if you don't get paid, we don't get paid" ones. It was ruled as an accident. I didn't even get so much as insurance money.

The results don't settle well with me to this day. Would a middle-class, white woman been ruled as an accident the same way that an uninsured black woman would be? I don't normally like to play the race card, but it is what it is.

46

Prisons are toured almost daily. Some are future staff, and some are juveniles on their scared straight/last chance tour. I've always been vocal and open about my life. I hope that my fuck ups will prevent the next guy's fuck ups.

Out of the thousands that I've spoken to, only two have come to me and said that they remembered me. Some groups are reluctant to ask questions. I've never denied answering any. The most memorable question was the one from the Brownies, you know, the baby Girl Scouts. They asked how to make dildos. I'm still floored by that one. What's wrong with our youth? Doesn't anyone play with dolls anymore?

North Carolina Travel and Tourism gives out travel information for those who call a 1-800 number. It is also trained inmates. I absolutely loved my job there. It was in a trailer that made you feel as though you weren't in prison.

One of the staff assigned there was Ma V. We began doing time around the same time. She was so funny and mild-mannered. I could sit at her feet and listen to her wisdom like a child in front of a fireplace.

She kept it real and a lot of people, especially her coworkers, were distant because of that. Oh well, I'm on it like this…keep it real or keep it movin'.

47

I'm creeping around with a chick that's younger than me named Afton. I was perfectly fine creeping around, but some folks just have to lay claim on you and that's usually when the shit goes south.

Afton was young and sometimes did dumb shit. We ended up getting caught having sex and went to lockup. We got separated living-wise once we got out and that was pretty much that.

Afton contacted me 10 years after she'd been released. She apologized for any harm she'd caused when she was younger. I let bygones be bygones these days. I thought that gesture was really nice. It's good to hear when people have their shit together.

48

I go to the infirmary every Friday to get my MS injection. I began to notice that this same person was always there. She was on reception and in a wheelchair. My nosiness couldn't help but to ask why she was in the wheelchair. Her name is Kina and she has MS. Oh, "Me too," I said. We aren't supposed to talk to people who aren't in regular population, so conversations were sparse.

The wheelchair was temporary, thankfully. When she stood, she was fucking tall as hell. Kina was beautiful. She's a Lane Bryant girl with green eyes and very smart. We had a lot in common and became close friends. She wanted to lose weight, so we'd walk every day, even longer on the weekends.

Kina didn't live together so we'd pass notes when we met up outside to catch each other up on the day and of course my craziness. I'm not normally blindsided but this really floored me. Kina and I had been friends for almost two years when the note she gave me confessed that she liked me. We were together a lot and people speculated that was the case anyway, but it wasn't.

Kina was different in the sense where she was with during my crazy shenanigans and didn't appear to like women. Well, she didn't, but she liked me. I loved her as my friend so why not cross over?

Kina eventually left, visited me, and did way more than people I'd known a lifetime. She eventually got married, had a baby, etc. Great for her, not for me. Realistically did I expect her to stick around for a lifetime? Well, maybe. She was different. I eventually stopped trying to contact her. Maybe she would've remained my friend, but I just couldn't stand the thought of her being married. Kinda selfish, huh?

The fast forward to that is that 12 years later Kina contacted me. If you love someone, you just love them, it's not a faucet that you can turn off and on. The dynamics of our lives have changed but we've made amends and are taking things one moment at the time.

49

We try to make the best of our shitty lives by celebrating birthdays and holidays. I don't usually partake in the groups, but I do use them as a day of reflection. Where do I see my life on this day? Free?

I miss my every day, not one specific one. I grieve the life that I live as well as the one I've lost. When I was younger, I'd make a list of things that I wanted from the canteen that coincided with my age. For my thirtieth birthday Kina got everything on the list. I stopped making lists after that. That was one of the many reasons that Kina was different and why our breakup, departure, or however you'll refer to it as was so devastating.

I do not know how this fairy tale ending was supposed to end. In my warped sense of reality perhaps it wasn't.

50

Another senseless death has occurred. A humble-spirited woman named Faye has died. Faye was incarcerated as long as I've been on this earth. As I'm writing this that makes 45 years. Yeah, that's what I said.

Faye was one of those who was in the wrong place at the wrong time. She did not physically kill anyone but was present. The person killed was law enforcement whose life appears to be worth more than unarmed black men. She'd beaten cancer once, only to have it return.

There was a pandemic of the coronavirus COVID-19. She died from complications due to her compromised immune system.

I hope that Faye is remembered for the positivity and humbleness that she exuded. I also hope that I don't end up like her…another death behind the wall. R.I.P. Faye.

51

Just when you think that you've gotten away with something, the boomerang of life shows its ugly head. I'll get to that shortly.

Kendra was a white chick that was going home soon—just the way I like it. I didn't fuck with (literally) long-termers. Who wants to be annoyed for years on end? We decided to have one last fling before she left.

What I didn't know was that I was being shipped to Southern Correctional Institution the following day. This wasn't a new prison, but it was new to women. It was a male prison that had been revamped for women because the female population was vastly expanding.

Some wanted a change and had requested to come to Southern but not me. I was perfectly content where I was. They kinda let me get away with murder and I was established, if you will. Why would I want to leave?

I showed my ass, cut the fool, and any phrase that refers to protesting, but guess what? My black ass was still made to take that bus ride.

I thought that I was settling down a little. I had even been looking at avenues to get the hell out of prison. I didn't know why I'd been chosen to move, and I was unhappy to say the least.

The first week was the toughest. The outside resembled Alcatraz and the inside didn't look much different. Everything was inside, i.e., gym, medical, chow. There would be no battling the weather to wander to and fro. There were no squirrels or trees. The cells are single with a button to push. I'm not claustrophobic but I wondered about how someone could get to me in case of an emergency. At 32 I had to reevaluate my surroundings and survival. What in the hell had I gotten into?

52

I do have the answer as to why I was shipped to Southern. Well...I was helping to clean out one of the rooms at the gym. Our job was to box the shit up and clean the room.

I was stripping and buffing floors when Kat, another one that we've lost along the way, called and said, "Say cheese." I struck a pose jokingly until I realized that she had literally snapped my picture. I was like, "Oh shit, you just snapped my picture!" No one used Polaroid anymore. She'd found a Polaroid camera with a couple of packs of film.

Sheila used to steal them back in the day and return to the store saying that they didn't fit her camera. Most stores didn't require a receipt and they were about $10 apiece. That's easy money. They also didn't used to chain fur and leather coats down. I believe that Sheila was the catalyst for that too.

Anyway, since no one (staff) knew about this camera, you might as well take the picture that you wanted, right? Pictures were taken in prison, but the poses were plain, i.e., no hand gestures, provocative poses, etc. Shit...YOLO. There were three of us, so we took turns taking poses. The other two were trying to be all bland and shit. I was like, fuck it. I took my clothes off. Yep, I posed naked on top of storage bins. I found some flowers that were props and got on the steps like a calendar girl and even took some selfies. I'm positive that I invented selfies.

We were sworn to send these pictures out. If we got caught, it would've been beyond our asses in lockup.

I slid a couple to this guy who was just a cutie that used to talk to me a lot, a chick that I was having a fling with that worked in the gym, and I flashed the camera for a pen pal website. Surely someone will want to write me then.

When the post returned for my approval, the assistant warden had it and asked me about it. I lied and denied that it was me. I swore that I'd been Photoshopped. Just when I thought that she bought it and all was settled they shipped me to Southern. I guess the case was settled for them.

Do you know they punished that prison for seven years and wouldn't allow them to take pictures? I think that they can only take bust shots now. Sorry guys....

53

The staff appear to be pleasant, but I don't give a shit because I do not want to be there. There were two guys that I would've fought on day one if I could've gotten away with it. I absolutely grew to love them, one more than the other. We may revisit that later.

The social worker was nice and told me about Family Day. She had been trained by Ma so she had no choice but to be a rose in this garden of thorns. Colt's a recent 18 and he can make his own choices, right? Maybe he'll want to come and spend the day with me.

Our social worker contacted his social worker, and I sent the information, and it was given to Colt. Karen got wind of this, called the social worker here and cussed Colt's case worker out. Really, bitch, he's 18. Karen tells them that I have no rights, they were terminated, etc. We know that was never the case and he'll be making his own decisions soon.

People told me that he would eventually come around, but I wasn't convinced. You never know how bad someone can poison you, especially a child.

This crushes my soul. I don't know why I'm not used to it by now. I guess that I expected Karen to ease up as Colt aged but boy, was I wrong. I'm defeated once again.

54

Prison is smokeless and cashless now which was implemented to reduce loansharking, bullying, etc. What it did was make us more creative. A convict has nothing but think time. It's gonna work two ways—for me and against you. It takes a minute to see how things are gonna work, who you can trust, fuck with, etc. I'd brought some money with me, but it was starting to look funny.

I had signed up for some pen-pal sites and luckily that threw me a lifeline. I had a pen-pal that looked out and was from Australia. I really liked him and hate that we no longer communicate. He was cool as hell. Damn, Stewart, where are you?

We also receive prepackaged boxes four times a year now. There's no more bringing food to visitation and we all wear state-issued clothes. They're irregular and make us look like a bunch of clones. They (the state) claim that it was more cost-effective than allowing us to receive our own clothes. The state will shoot you a hot lie in a minute and always imply that it's best for us. What the state constantly does is try to belittle you and rape you of your self-esteem. If you are not strong, I guarantee that you will leave more broken than you came.

55

Dee was one of my friends who had a crazy boyfriend who held a gun to her head and drove the getaway car. What choice did she have? Eight years is the choice that the state gave her.

Dee had the most wonderful parents who thought highly of me. I didn't have anyone to send me these care package boxes and they got mine. They didn't get one box a year, they got all four for several years even after Dee was released. I called Ma and Pa. I still talk to them, call them, and Ma writes sending prayers daily. I'm so fortunate to have come across what real family is supposed to look like.

Pa is sickly these days and that breaks my heart. Good people do not deserve bad. Life sucks sometimes.

Knowledge is power. It's the only thing that's truly yours and that no one can take from you. Southern offers a degree program and I'm coming for it.

I had tried to obtain a degree in the past with the college that NCCIW was affiliated with. If you had more than 10 years you could not obtain the free education. You could get a sponsor or someone to pay for it for you.

KAIROS is a religious retreat full of nonjudgmental people who want to share agape. I began KAIROS at age 19 and have maintained a connection with many of them along the way.

Gen was an ex-inmate who attended a Native church. Volunteers come and go so this was great that someone from her church wanted to have pastoral visits with me. It wouldn't hurt. The pastor visited faithfully and along the way asked what I wanted, minus freedom, of course. I explained that I've always wanted a degree. He offered to pay for my education via his church!

OMG! I was so excited. Everyone who knew me was just as excited as me. I enrolled, went to class, etc. About two weeks into the semester the principal called me to her office. She was a big butch of a woman who never smiled, but for some reason she was humble. She explained that the money had not been turned in for me and didn't know what to do. I figured that there was a delay or mix up and turned my books in, vowing to retrieve them soon.

I talked to the pastor a lot prior to this. What happened? He didn't take my calls, he never visited again. WTF?

56

A lawyer who I'd come across had entered my life by now. Her name is Kate. She became a lawyer at age 40 and switched the type of law she practiced after meeting me. She still works with juveniles and that's been 15 years ago. After about two months of trying, Kate caught up with him. He'd been promoted and gone to another church and has supposedly left someone else in charge of handling school. Kate said that he seemed embarrassed and apologetic, as well he should've been. It's another example of being so close to something yet so far away.

57

The gym is better than NCCIW and they have a service club. The yard and ballfield are also spacious. Running is permitted and I can take advantage of that. I didn't realize that I enjoyed it as much as I do and how much endurance I have. Running is my think time. I've even run a couple of half-marathons already. I plan to run for those with MS who can't. I want them to sponsor me while I run to bring awareness. Sounds good, right?

I join the service club and am elected as treasurer. Why not? I've been a CPA for several years—certified prison accountant. On the weekends I chill with my new friends Tarra and Danielle. We have children similar in age and have a lot in common. We talk about what the kids would be doing, what we'd be doing if we were free, and eat the occasional pint of ice cream. Sherbet is my jam!

It was Mother's Day weekend, Sunday to be exact. Visitation was going on and none of us had one. I rarely had them anyway. My little sister Jessica lived close, and she would visit on occasion. Sandy had two daughters by Elvetha, Maria, and Jessica. I actually named Jessica. I'm 14 years older than her. She and Colt are less than two years apart. I guess I had a little girl before I had a little boy.

Tarra pointed out that they'd called my name, the PA's on repeat. Good thing it is because I didn't hear it the first time.

I rush to get my picture tickets. I try to keep two for just-in-cases. I also keep a freshly ironed outfit. I am grateful that Jessica came but why choose such a busy day to come? Maybe she's out of work.

I'm scanning the crowded room looking for Jessica. It's packed like sardines which means an extra long wait time for a strip search. As I'm making one more scan someone steps from behind the soda machines and says, "It's me."

58

Colt truly surprised me. It was beyond emotional. I remember the day as if it was yesterday. It was hard to catch up on all of the years that we'd been separated but we damn sure tried.

He told me of his plans for the future which consisted of the military. The Marines interested him the most. It kinda fits because of the strength he already possessed.

Although the thought of it terrified me, I gave him my blessing and support. It seemed as though the moment that I got him back, life had stolen him again. He's ready to take on the world and get the hell away from Karen. Who can blame him? We have several visits until the fall when he begins boot camp.

We took a couple of pictures that I treasure to this day. I don't know who was smiling harder, me or him. The adults in my life had always told me that he would return but I had a hard time believing them. I guess they didn't get to be that age and not know what they were talking about.

59

There are a lot of annoying things about prison life. I cannot narrow it down to one but count time is in the top three. We're counted at least four times a day. Where in the hell could we have gone?

The barbed wire is intense, and the fences are gravitational and high. Besides, we're women. We don't generally try to escape. Don't get me wrong, there have been some.

Shirley was a wild child who'd done a lot of time and had at least seven more years to go. She had a girlfriend named Busala with long, black hair and a friend named Suki.

They had the bright idea of escaping one morning. Shirley had got over the fence. Suki got over the fence. Busala's black Rapunzel locks got stuck and they had to go back to get her.

Okay, first of all, who tries to be cute during an escape? Secondly, if I'm free, you.are.on.your.own. I wouldn't have gone back for anyone. Deuces!

But don't worry, there's always a good Samaritan that screams and points saying, "You've got two on the fence, you've got two on the fence!" It's a good thing that they transferred the snitch because

Shirley had a history of fighting inmates and staff.

The snitch ended up at honor grade way before she was eligible. The three amigos spent two years in lockup. That shit will make you lose your mind. No human contact for two years, the same four-by-four cell. Fuck that!

The law regarding solitary confinement only allows you to do 30 days at a time without a 24-hour break. It was only considered inhumane after they let some guy serve 13 years. Cruel and unusual punishment is an understatement.

The other escape wasn't as dramatic. Joy hid in a dumpster until nightfall and was picked up by her boyfriend. She had an inside accomplice who'd made her bed to give the illusion of a body.

They counted and counted and recounted for two days. We couldn't go anywhere or do anything. The bitch is gone, SUCK IT UP! The accomplice went to segregation for a year or two. Joy stayed gone for seven years. I don't know what the record is but I think that's impressive. She was caught in another state and of course had to return to finish out her sentence.

Oh yeah, this is one more annoying, degrading thing that occurs here—a urinalysis a.k.a. piss test. They're "random" supposedly unless you have a history of drug use.

You must squat, cough, and then squat over the toilet with one hand on the wall, the other holding the cup, and with some God-awful staff eye level to your snatch.

Those who are "dirty" come prepared with clean piss inside of them. That thang ain't called a pocketbook for no reason. In case of emergency, it can hold some shit. I've never done drugs which is why these tests are particularly annoying for me. Welcome to my "random" world.

60

Let's talk about this food. I don't know what you've heard, but it ain't five-star. It hasn't killed me, obviously, and I prefer it as opposed to canteen because it has vegetables. But they are often overcooked and mushy.

I've had a fly in the middle of my roll. I've had crickets in my greens and rocks in my pintos. Expect the occasional hair that you know is from some stringy-haired white girl, and don't expect the lipstick to be completely removed from your glasses.

I'm a soup person but I was spared botulism when my friend Phaedra told me not to eat the soup. Why? Because Octavia had put a rat in the soup pot on some get-back shit. Aren't rats a delicacy somewhere? I'm guessing not in prison.

The nasty shit is what they serve the most of. Hamburger yakisoba. What in the hell is that? The hamburger looks as dry as the fake soba noodles.

Baked beans are only pintos with sugar on them. Pineapple coleslaw. Why? Fiesta coleslaw—that has tomatoes and celery. Some Mexican is turning over in his grave. Turkey a la king. Ain't nothing on a cart. Cheese is often a no-meat substitute. I eat it even though it doesn't melt. They even have veggie burgers that are light skinned, square, and dry as hell. People call them cardboard. They're choke burgers but I eat them too. My oatmeal and grits are runny which pisses me off. They try to stretch the food by adding water to it. Yuck! But all of that is periodically tolerable. What isn't and will never be is a black-eyed pea. Damn, they're nasty. Even you that eat them know that they taste like dirt. How can y'all eat them thangs?

A lot of inmates are overweight. It isn't because of the above but due to the biscuits, rolls, desserts, and noodles from the canteen. A noodle is roughly 25 cents. It'll fill you up, it's cheap, and even if you don't get money, you can bum a noodle from the world's biggest asshole. And for some reason, inmates are sedentary saying they'll lose weight when they get out. Crack and meth do work but walking a lap or two wouldn't hurt them.

61

I utilize our gym and stay outside until they make me come in. Shit, I'm 35 and 40 isn't far away. Will it be all downhill from there?

I have a new job now, I'm a hair technician. By looking at me you'd never know that I have a license in cosmetology. My hair is usually in a ponytail or braided. I work out a lot, therefore I sweat a lot. My hair is to the middle of my back, there aren't many options.

I like people transforming before my eyes with each hairstyle or haircut. They're my human baby dolls. The only drawback is that my boss is a bitch. She's a little, short, dumpy witch who's also my unit manager. She had an orange jacket once that was too small. I nicknamed her Pumpkin, behind her back, of course.

And as always, someone came along to disrupt my life. She was cute, kinda crazy, and a lot jealous. The last two came as a surprise. But I hadn't had a girlfriend since Kina which was four years prior, so I thought why not?

Nino and I were good until she started accusing me of the guy who worked in the gym which was the guy that I mentioned at the beginning of my Southern trip that I said that we might revisit.

Nino didn't know for sure, but she raised enough stink and allegations that closed the entire gym down for seven months. Ugh!

The fast forward is that she went home, contacted me, and even puts money on my phone account from time to time. At least she's useful now.

62

Prison has a lot of lulls. The faces change, your emotions are on a constant rollercoaster, but the bullshit remains the same. As you age, the drama becomes less oooh, aaaah, and your give-a-damn gets busted. That's where I am. I'm just letting life do what it do.

I try to fill my time positively and one of the things that I do is take photos at visitation for our service club. Two of us go to take the tickets and pictures. We sit and narrate the visitors that we haven't seen. It breaks the monotony.

As we were leaving, one of the male visitors spoke to me. We're not technically supposed to talk but you don't want to be rude either. This gentleman was visiting one of my hair clients.

After visitation Christy said that her stepdad asked about me and wanted to write. Sure, I had nothing to do and no one significant in my life at this point.

The more that Tommy, Christy's stepdad, communicated, the more I liked him. He was quite a bit older, but he had a lot of swag. Tommy reminded me of Aaron but in a distinguished way, not a grandpa way.

I hate to use this phrase, but Tommy became my sugar daddy. He visited, sent money, and I could call him. I've not been able to call that many people on a consistent basis, so this was nice. Maybe the universe was lightening up for me.

Tommy is by far the sweetest man I've ever met. He wants the best for everyone and is exceptionally kind. Tommy asks me to marry him and I accept.

63

Let me tell you a funny story right quick. I was the rector for KAIROS the previous year. Around the time that we were planning, there was something called a marriage seminar going on in the same building.

The chaplain was killing two birds with one stone and invited the KAIROS planner to partake of a few snacks from the seminar. I spoke with a couple and jokingly said that I was gonna rent a husband for the following one because the seminar looked really nice. It was a relaxed setting that looked really cozy and inviting.

And even though you're in prison, chances are you matter to someone, whether it be a mother, wife, or friend.

I'm looking forward to getting married even though I think it's the scariest thing I've ever done in my life. Yeah, me. Scared shitless! I don't have any examples of marriage working and I don't really pride myself of being the marrying type. And besides, the last person I loved got me a life sentence. Can you see my reluctance?

I saw a dress in the newspaper which was only about 20 minutes from where Tommy lived. I was even gonna look the part. Wow!

So, on November 9, 2012, also my thirty-seventh birthday, I

married Tommy.

For a prison wedding, I'd say that it went well. I'd never been to a wedding before, so I had nothing to compare it to. Paul, Tommy's oldest brother, and my lawyer friend Kris were our witnesses.

I met Kris about 25 years ago. She handled some legal issues in the beginning of my case, and we've remained close ever since. She has been one of my biggest champions and supporters for pretty much my entire sentence. I'd definitely take a bullet for her.

64

Colt is in the middle of Timbuktu by now. He's active military but we communicate when we can. He also visits when he's in the states. I've sent him a picture of me in my wedding dress; I hope he gets it.

It's December and Colt's home for Christmas. Yeah! He surprises me by popping up for visitation. It's Colt that gets the surprise because Tommy's already sitting in visitation in another section.

We all sit together as a blended family. SURPRISE! Colt is polite and reserved. It was just us for so long and here I am with this new stranger.

Tommy is one of those people who are impossible not to like, so over time Colt becomes more receptive of the idea. Over time they both give me hell simultaneously. Did I really sign up for this?

Tommy's a Vietnam vet with PTSD. It's gotten 1,000 percent better, but I think it's fucked up that resources were not in place for them back then.

One of the most admirable things that Tommy does is care for his almost-100-year-old mother. I met her once prior to getting married. She barely came up to my shoulder, but she was the most adorable person that I ever did see. She's spry and talks shit. Man, I hope that's me at her age.

65

From the time that I entered prison, I was ready to go. It ain't my home. I ain't staking claim on none of this shit and I hate it with every fiber of my being. Some are so institutionalized that they have to sit at the same table and chair every day. They really get an attitude and are ready to fight if anything is out of place. Man, they can have this shit. Ain't none of it on my inventory and I'm taking very little when I go.

I've begged for help, writing or calling anyone that I've met along the way who I thought could help. If I could at the least get my sentences to run concurrently, I'd have won the war.

Tommy has hired an attorney in hopes to expedite my freedom. It's easy to get in and hard as hell to get out. I've had this attorney for several years without any recourse thus far.

The laws concerning how juveniles are sentenced have been enacted. In hindsight they indirectly affect my case. We're filing something and moving forward.

Some of the juvenile and prison reform advocates have begun to contact, that's a switch. There are several who want me to share my story in hopes to gain awareness and recognition towards my release.

I'm on the news first. I believe that the interview went well but after looking at myself, why didn't someone stop me from wearing that blue eyeshadow?

I've done an episode for "For My Man." People have viewed it and contacted me. I've done some radio interviews with the Pink Peacock Project. A woman named Sara has been a big help. The Beat 139 has also been an integral part of raising awareness for my situation. I have so much for me, who could be against me? As great as it sounds, there's still several assholes who say, "Let her in." "She's done the crime, let her do the time." The haters have always been my motivators and they'll always exist, so bring 'em on. I can only show you that success is my greatest revenge.

66

Sandy's out of prison and has become friends with Tommy. He and Colt have even formed somewhat of a bond. Tommy's older than Sandy. Most guess the opposite when guessing which is my husband.

Sandy's spent the majority of my life behind bars, but he's never lied or mistreated me the way that Sheila did. My biggest issue is that Sandy never grew up. Maybe if I'd have had a dad my life would've been different. He still lights up the room and there's never a dull moment. It's hard to miss a 300-pound Indian with green eyes.

I got fired from being a hair tech for cutting someone's hair too short. There are guidelines that we must follow. I actually didn't break them, she got her hair cut shorter on the yard. I had the proof but fuck it! What should've happened was that the chick should've gotten a blanket party.

What's that? For those who are outright ratchet and think they can get away with it, a group of folks throw a blanket on the person and beat them with a bunch of locks in socks. Oh yeah, that's real. It isn't just something that you see on TV. Sometimes people need to know that they're not untouchable.

I have a new job washing clothes. The perk with that is that I can wash my own whenever I want and not on designated days. You learn a lot when you wash someone's clothes.

The cute girls have the dirtiest drawers. It's as if they pile makeup on their face and no soap on their ass. The big gals have a tendency to have the whitest crotches. Ain't that ass-backwards?

67

Life at Southern Correctional lasted 10 years. I gained a lot of education, a few muscles, and hopefully a shorter path to freedom. I finally got the job that I always wanted…the gym. I had it less than six months, but I took full advantage of it.

The male population had become extremely violent. They went on a spree of killing each other and staff. In order to combat their mess, the females had to be shifted around in order to break them up. Several male prisons and the only two that they had for medium custody women.

We were supposed to be at Neuse Correctional Institution for a few months, but we ended up staying for a little over a year. It was an open quad that was not ready for the female population. It was actually a minimum/medium camp so there were a few more perks than usual.

The air was hot. It rained the whole time. The buildings had mold and it was full of spiders when we got there. God, it took forever to get the place inhabitable. There were no washers and dryers like we were accustomed to. The clothes house sent whatever size they had to replace what you turned in.

We eventually made clotheslines and washed out clothes by hand. I don't know if this exists but I'm sure that our place resembled a ghetto, Mexican trailer park in a third world country. But you know what? We made do.

There were no jobs or classes except a handful. I got a CPCA certificate—certified personal care aide. The nurse who taught it was awesome. I learned a lot. I did even get a job towards the end of my stay at the clothes house. I wish that I'd have gotten it sooner because I loved my bosses.

The warden was cooler than a fan and down to earth. He'd pop in any given moment and chop it up with you.

68

But with the make-dos came a lot of make-don'ts. People worked off site and you had staff trying to make a buck, so the drugs were prevalent. You name it and they had it. This year was a much-needed break for those of us who'd done a lot of time.

People who hadn't done drugs ever or in a while did them. Sometimes there were so many that folks gave them away. No, I didn't do any, but I sure made some money off of them. Hell, somebody was gonna do it, it might as well have been me.

The staff were cool and very laid back also. Everything went and with that I'm gonna have to take that story to the grave. A friend Kate and I used to say that we were gonna write a book about "How I Survived Neuse." It was a great year. Damn, I miss it!

69

I want to make sure that you have the most accurate description of my life and its surroundings. The prisons may change but the generalities are the same.

Six a.m. shift change, 6:30 a.m. breakfast, 8 a.m. work/yard, 11 a.m. lunch, 12 p.m. count, 1 p.m. yard/back to work, 3:30 p.m. dinner, 5 p.m. count, 6 p.m. shift change/yard may reopen/ evening classes, 8 p.m. yard closed. Somewhere between 9 and 11 p.m. count. Somewhere around 12 a.m. lights out. Isn't that the most awful routine to replay daily? It's Groundhog Day on repeat.

I did make it to honor grade once. Don't get excited. It was a fluke. While at Neuse, we had a hurricane and those who built the prison didn't take into account that one could ever happen, so it was built in a floodplain. Genius.

The entire prison was evacuated and sent to local prisons for a couple of weeks. The prison was already being revamped for men, but the yard was spacious. I liked that. What I didn't like was the fact that the grass hadn't been cut in God knows how long and the mosquitos were the size of my butt cheeks. Our bites had bites. Ugh!

After about three weeks we returned unharmed and thankfully our belongings that remained behind unharmed. We don't have much i.e., a few pictures, letters, or something silly. It doesn't matter to anyone but us. You'd probably disregard it as junk. Just know that one man's junk is truly another man or woman's treasure.

70

As you can guess I've seen and done a lot by this point. I've been regarded as being strong. I don't always agree with that adjective. Maybe I'm just too nosy to give up. What if I die and I was really close to the end? That would suck.

There are some and more these days than before who cannot handle their time. The crazy part is that they're not usually long-termers and damn sure not lifers.

There was a girl who lived in a mental health dorm. You'd think that they'd be monitored more closely than others but prison's always short staffed. And quite frankly, we're just smarter than them. We have 24 hours a day, seven days a week to plot. Staff only has 12 hours at best to see what we've plotted about.

Nicole timed the staff's rounds and hung herself in between them. Simple as that. Someone in lockup jumped from atop one of the cages. Ouch! I do not know how she climbed up there, but she did. There was another in lockup who hung herself. The ones who hung themselves were with sheets. The officer that found her couldn't recover after that. She literally cut this lifeless body down. She draws disability now for PTSD. Maybe it only affects the ones who care and aren't here just for a paycheck.

71

On a lighter note, the first gay marriage was performed at Neuse. I told you that they let us get away with shit. That really wasn't a big deal or at least it shouldn't have. The couple had to get the news and protesters involved. Well, damn! Now another prison is remembered for yet another form of hatred and prejudice. Life on the inside doesn't get any better than this.

72

I've had a couple of really low points in my life. Shocker, right? I didn't try suicide or anything. I don't want to fuck the people that I'd leave behind, especially Colt. So, I turned my pain into words that will hopefully help those who can relate.

I wrote a meditative journal titled "31 Days of Growth and Reflection". I believe that you can make a change in a month's time. I'm a big proponent of journaling. I find it extremely therapeutic. I also want the world to know what I really thought when I'm gone. Colt teases me and says, "Uh uh, that's (my journal) going with you!"

I also wrote "Memoirs of Suzie". It's a short story about the relationship that I had with Sheila. We matched up as good as a sausage and peanut sandwich would.

My life is not ideal but on many levels I'm still more fortunate than some who are free. Would I trade with any of them at their lowest? Absolutely. I would rise above knowing that I was not surrounded by bars, barbed wire, the same outfit, a TV that I could not change when I wanted to, and of course, <u>no count times</u>!

73

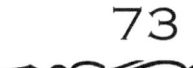

The prison where the women were intended finally opened. The name was Lanesboro even though it was renamed as Anson Correctional Institution. The male inmates were fighting the staff left and right. I don't know what this place looked like before they fixed it up for us but there are still several rooms that are uninhabitable. The windows looked like they've been shot out. I don't know how they got broken.

A fresh coat of paint cannot hide the black soot underneath the desks. We're told that those were "cook" rooms. What did they start the fires with? You'd think that the staff would be glad that they don't have to fight for their lives. A lot of them still have the male population mentality and antagonize us. They're quick to say, "The men did this, the men did that." The day that they had to order tampons and sanitary pads nixed it being a male facility.

Women are more manipulative. We do not have to fight you to get what we want. We'd rather fuck with your money, reputation, and livelihood by calling PREA. That's an acronym for Prison Rape Something Something. All I have to do is call PREA and your ass is under investigation, not getting a promotion, and/or out of a job. Fuck with me if you want to.

74

We have a female warden who we had at Southern. The bitch forgot that she knew us. You cannot give black women a lot of power at times. It really goes to their head. I know that sounds racist as hell, but the shit is real. We don't have a lot of programs or activities and we've been here almost a year. Anson was not ready to house women.

On top of everything else, the world is under a pandemic. Seriously, COVID-19 is taking place. You don't even usually see one in a lifetime. I hope this is my one and only. One of the things that keeps a pandemic at bay is socially distancing. That is impossible to do in prison. We do the best that we can with what we have to work with, but will it be enough to weather the storm? We've lost so many lives due to this disease already. The state refuses to release those with compromised immune systems and those who've served an extensive amount of years, such as myself.

75

I've served 31 years thus far. I hope that the state will agree that that's enough. Until I'm free, I'll continue to find my few joys in life like a clear blue sky and jelly beans. They're both my favorite. I'm also gonna sit in half lotus and share my words with the world. I hope that you never enter my world but fight for me to reenter into yours. Until then…namaste.

My Son

Locked away without your smile is the worse imprisonment that you can imagine.

The hole in my heart at times is more than you can fathom.

You've grown from baby to boy and now boy to man.

I've parented from afar—I hope you know that I've done the best that I can.

I am proud of you. You are different and more special than the others.

No words can express just how much I love being your mother.

I love you, babe.

April Barber

(This is the poem that I won an open mic with.)

Acknowledgements

It's impossible to give a shout out to everyone who's mattered to me in these almost 45 years of life, but I'll try....

Everyone that I spoke to, staff and inmates, at NCCIW, Southern Correctional, Neuse Correctional, and Anson Correctional. Those who sent money to me, a little or a lot. I needed it. I appreciated it and I hope to see you one day. To those who tried to help with my case along the way i.e., lawyer, prison reform, or advocacy group. Please continue the good fight. For those that I shared a piece of my heart with...I still do. If I ever said, "I love you," know that it is true.

Tommy, the person who saw something different in me enough to want to give me your last name...wow! It's still unbelievable. And Colt...this time is so much easier with you in my life, and I'd have it no other way.

ABOUT THE AUTHOR

    April Scales may be one of the most profound inmates that's ever served time. She entered the system at age 15 but continues to better herself while fighting for her freedom.

    April has accomplished more in her incarcerated lifetime than many do that are free. She continuously proves that you can lock a person's body away but not their mind or their will to change.

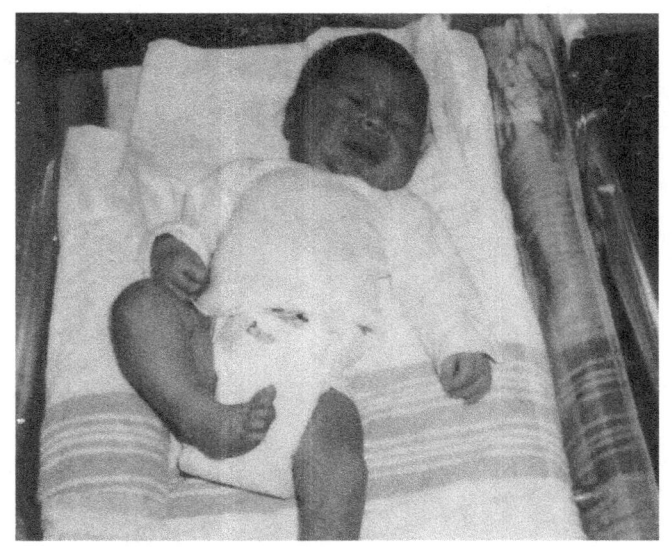

Colt when he was born.
Wasn't he big as hell?

Me & Jessica
My Li'l Sis

Me & Peaches

My old pen pal Stuart.
I made ths sweater.

Kris (My lawyer friend), Tommy, Me, and Paul (Tommy's brother)

Me & Tommy

My mother-in-law
Isn't she the cutest thing
you ever did see?

Me & Sandy - Yeah, we're twins.

I love my baby!

He's such a big kid.

They grow up
so fast!

I'm proud of my books.

www.ingramcontent.com/pod-product-compliance
Lightning Source LLC
Chambersburg PA
CBHW071852070526
44583CB00016B/1648